First Person
A ★ M ★ E ★ R ★ I ★ C ★ A

THE NATION IN TURMOIL

Civil Rights and the Vietnam War (1960-1973)

Gene Brown

Twenty-First Century Books

A Division of Henry Holt and Company
New York

Twenty-First Century Books
A Division of Henry Holt and Company, Inc.
115 West 18th Street
New York, New York 10011

Henry Holt® and colophon are trademarks of Henry Holt and Company, Inc.
Publishers since 1866

Published in Canada by Fitzhenry & Whiteside Ltd.
195 Allstate Parkway, Markham, Ontario L3R 4T8

Printed in the United States of America
All first editions are printed on acid-free paper ∞.

Created and produced in association with Blackbirch Graphics, Inc.

Library of Congress Cataloging-in-Publication Data

Brown, Gene.
    The nation in turmoil: civil rights and the Vietnam War, 1960–1973 / Gene Brown.— 1st edition.
        p.   cm. — (First person America)
    Includes bibliographical references and index.
    Summary: Presents primary source materials covering such major social and political events in United States history as the civil rights movement, the Great Society, and the Vietnam War and anti-war sentiment.
    ISBN 0-8050-2588-X (alk. paper)
    1. United States—History—1961–1969—Sources—Juvenile literature.
2. Vietnamese Conflict, 1961–1975—Sources—Juvenile literature. 3. Civil rights movements—United States— History— 20th century—Sources—Juvenile literature. 4. United States—History—1969– —Sources—Juvenile literature [1. United States—History—1969– —Sources. 2. United States—Social conditions—1960–1980—Sources.] I. Title. II. Series.
E841.B74   1993
973.92—dc20   93-24995
                                                                      CIP
                                                                       AC

CONTENTS

INTRODUCTION

Of all the decades in the recent past, few stir the passions of Americans more than the 1960s and early 1970s. Even today, people still debate the events of this era. Was this a golden age of idealism, when the country took big steps toward ending poverty and prejudice? Or were they years in which old values were destroyed without being replaced by anything else? Was it a time of the growth of freedom in many areas of life? Or was it when the growth of government got out of hand and threatened freedom?

America began the 1960s with a young president, John F. Kennedy. He came to stand for a new energy among young people, a desire to do meaningful public service, and a commitment to change the world for the better. Many college students of the time wanted more than a job after school. The president offered them an opportunity to serve their country—and the people of other nations—by creating the Peace Corps. JFK's vision of what America could and should do was far-reaching: He even began the race to put a man on the moon.

Many Americans of all ages and races went to work in the civil rights movement that took shape in the early 1960s. African Americans had begun pushing for their rights on a large scale during the 1950s. By the early 1960s, they were challenging segregation in the South on all fronts with freedom rides and sit-ins.

Dr. Martin Luther King, Jr. became the symbol of what could be done if people stood up to hatred and bigotry.

For most Americans, the 1960s were prosperous. Since World War II, the United States had experienced almost constant economic growth. Incomes kept rising. The American standard of living was the world's highest and kept improving. Every generation, it seemed, could look forward to a better life than the previous one had.

More Americans were going to college than ever before. Confident that they would be able to earn a good living when it became necessary, millions of young people had the freedom to think about how they wanted to live before facing the pressures of jobs and families. They had the chance to question some of the ideas with which they were brought up. Many did this, and the results were not always to their parents' liking.

Demonstrators marched from Selma, Alabama, to the State Capitol in Montgomery in 1965 to focus attention on the civil rights movement (© *Bob Adelman, Magnum*).

Jacqueline Kennedy leads her children down the steps of the White House on the way to the funeral of John F. Kennedy, November 25, 1963 (*National Archives*).

The assassination of President Kennedy in 1963 shocked Americans who had hoped that a great age of progress was dawning. The shootings of Martin Luther King, Jr. and Robert Kennedy in 1968 only strengthened the growing feeling of uneasiness. It seemed anything could happen; nothing and no one was safe from the political passions that swirled around civil rights, poverty, and the war in Vietnam.

But there was still some hope. In fact, President Lyndon B. Johnson's "Great Society" enacted programs that John F. Kennedy had not been able to get passed, such as Medicare and antipoverty measures. However positive the goals of these programs, they upset many Americans, who saw their taxes rise to pay for them.

Energized by the civil rights movement, college students began to protest against a wide range of things. Despite the relatively good times, nuclear war remained a constant threat. The testing of atom bombs above ground produced radioactivity that could spread and cause terrible harm. Some of it was getting into cows' milk and was then being absorbed by children.

The Cuban missile crisis of 1962, which pushed the United States and the Soviet Union to the brink of nuclear war, brought home the dangers of atomic weapons. Such a war could literally destroy the world in a matter of days. This sobering thought made many reconsider the need for these weapons and the use of war as a realistic way to settle conflicts.

The Vietnam War caused opposition to the government's foreign policy on a wide scale. President Johnson was steadily bombing strategic areas in Vietnam and sending more American troops each month, no matter how much people were opposed to these actions. This lack of response to orderly protest provoked the protestors to become more disruptive. Civil disobedience became increasingly popular.

Much of white, older, middle-class America did not like the antiwar protests. They also disapproved of the counterculture that seemed linked to the antiwar movement. Young men with long hair, the freer sexual behavior that seemed to be everywhere, and the widespread use of marijuana all angered "the older generation." Their belief was that young America was simply running wild.

Added to these major social changes was fear. Crime was rising in the cities, and some white Americans, looking at the large number of poor blacks being arrested, began to blame many urban problems on African Americans. The riots that seemed to heat up every summer in the mid-1960s only magnified these feelings. Some white Americans did not understand the connection between crime and poverty and did not fully consider the mistreatment that African Americans had suffered throughout our history.

Other major social changes began to take hold in the early 1970s. New equal rights movements for both women and homosexuals gained momentum and sparked nationwide debates that continue to this day. In addition to social upheaval, Americans also suffered economic hardship during the 1970s. The drastic and sudden rise in fuel prices caused by a coordinated effort from the world's major oil-producing nations (OPEC) created great economic problems. Swiftly rising inflation and recession also threatened to undermine the American standard of living.

In 1972, the Watergate scandal created a nationwide mistrust of government that, to this day, has not been completely overcome.

In many ways, Americans are still dealing with the legacy of these years. There is still much work to be done to eliminate racial injustice and poverty, and to create a government that inspires its people to action.

Women march down the streets of New York City during a rally for the proposed Equal Rights Amendment of the early 1970s (*Wide World Photos*).

CHAPTER 1

EXPLORING THE "NEW FRONTIER"

F

The Kennedy Legacy

ew presidential inauguration addresses are memorable enough to inspire a generation. The inaugural speech of John F. Kennedy (1917-1963) is probably the most often quoted since President Franklin D. Roosevelt's (1882–1945) inaugural speech in 1933. Roosevelt took office at a time of great anxiety, when the American economy was collapsing. The nation was desperate for a leader who could get the country out of trouble, and they listened carefully to FDR in hope that he would be that leader.

Kennedy was president in calmer times. President Eisenhower (1890–1969), whom Kennedy succeeded, had been very popular, mainly because he presided over a quiet period that followed the turmoil of the Depression and World War II. But as Kennedy sensed, a new generation was coming of age that had not experienced those difficult times. These younger people looked around and saw problems that were not being faced, such as poverty at home and abroad, and the denial of equal rights to certain groups of American

John Fitzgerald Kennedy
(*National Portrait Gallery*).

citizens. America's youth was idealistic and wanted a chance to help change the world for the better.

Kennedy had a talent for inspiring people. Although he didn't write the speech excerpted here (his speechwriter Ted Sorenson did), the ideas and the message were Kennedy's. The new president delivered the speech with such conviction that Americans across the nation were touched and moved to action. In fact, almost immediately, thousands volunteered for the Peace Corps, one of Kennedy's first major programs as president.

Today we remember President Kennedy more for his inspirational leadership than for particular accomplishments. He might have accomplished more in a second term, but his 1963 assassination ended that possibility.

A New President Speaks

Let the word go forth from this time and place, to friend and foe alike, that the torch has been passed to a new generation of Americans—born in this century, tempered by war, disciplined by a hard and bitter peace, proud of our ancient heritage—and unwilling to witness or permit the slow undoing of those human rights to which this nation has always been committed, and to which we are committed today at home and around the world.

Let every nation know, whether it wishes us well or ill, that we shall pay any price, bear any burden, meet any hardship, support any friend, oppose any foe to assure the survival and the success of liberty.

This much we pledge—and more.

To those old allies whose cultural and spiritual origins we share, we pledge the loyalty of faithful friends. United, there is little we cannot do in a host of new cooperative ventures. Divided, there is little we can do—for we dare not meet a powerful challenge at odds and split asunder. . . .

To those peoples in the huts and villages of half the globe struggling to break the binds of mass misery, we pledge our best efforts to help them help themselves, for whatever period is required—not because the communists may be doing it, not because we seek their votes, but because it is right. If a free society cannot help the many who are poor, it cannot save the few who are rich.

To our sister republics south of our border, we offer a special pledge—to convert our good words into good deeds—in a new alliance for progress—to assist free men and free governments in casting off the chains of poverty. But this peaceful revolution of hope cannot become the prey of hostile powers. Let all our neighbors know that we shall join with them to oppose aggression or subversion anywhere in the Americas. And let every other power know that this Hemisphere intends to remain the master of its own house. . . .

In the long history of the world, only a few generations have been granted the role of defending freedom in its hour of maximum danger. I do not shrink from this responsibility—I welcome it. I do not believe that any of us would exchange places with any other people or any other generation. The energy, the faith, the devotion which we bring to this endeavor will light our country and all who serve it—and the glow from that fire can truly light the world.

And so, my fellow Americans: ask not what your country can do for you—ask what you can do for your country.

From: John F. Kennedy, Inaugural Address, January 20, 1961, Washington, D.C.

Trying to Change America

One of the most important student activist groups of the early 1960s was Students for a Democratic Society, also known as SDS. Tom Hayden, the group's leading figure, was the editor of the student newspaper at the University of Michigan and participated in civil rights activities.

In 1962, a group of 59 members of SDS met at Port Huron in Michigan and adopted what became known as the Port Huron Statement. An excerpt from the statement, written by Hayden, is reprinted here. The document said that the clash between American ideals and the true conditions under which people lived in this country was causing many young people to lose their sense of connection to a real community. People were withdrawing from social action and they were trying their best to get satisfaction from their private lives. There was an atmosphere of what became known as "alienation."

SDS and this statement hit the right chord with many young people. The organization became influential mostly in white students' activities to protest the Vietnam War and in efforts to reform universities and colleges in America.

As the 1960s went on, and the government and other institutions resisted change, new leadership took over SDS. Slowly, the group turned toward more direct action and finally, to violence. Splits occurred in which one group of SDS would denounce another. As its

SDS leader Tom Hayden testifies before Congress in 1968 (*Wide World Photos*).

organization weakened, SDS's influence declined. But the more isolated it became, the more extreme it got. Finally, it was reduced to a small band of outlaws, some of whom finally went to prison for their actions.

The early members of SDS went on to other things. Tom Hayden continued to work for change and is now a member of the California Legislature.

A Call to Action

When we were kids the United States was the wealthiest and strongest country in the world; the only one with the atom bomb, the least scarred by modern war, an initiator of the United Nations that we thought would distribute Western influence throughout the world. Freedom and equality for each individual, government of, by, and for the people—these American values we found good, principles by which we could live as men.

As we grew, however, our comfort was penetrated by events too troubling to dismiss. First, fact of human degradation, symbolized by the Southern struggle against racial bigotry, compelled most of us from silence to activism. Second, the enclosing fact of the Cold War, symbolized by the presence of the Bomb, brought awareness that we ourselves, and our friends, and millions of abstract "others" we knew more directly because of our common peril, might die at any time.

While two-thirds of mankind suffers undernourishment, our own upper classes revel amidst superfluous abundance. Although world population is expected to double in forty years, the nations still tolerate anarchy as a major principle of international conduct and uncontrolled exploitation governs the sapping of the earth's physical resources. Although mankind desperately needs revolutionary leadership, America rests in national stalemate, its goals ambiguous and tradition-bound instead of informed and clear, its democratic system apathetic and manipulated rather than "of, by, and for the people."

From: *SDS Port Huron Statement*, (reprinted in *The New Radicals*), 1962.

CHAPTER 2

"WE SHALL OVERCOME"

The Struggle for Equality

Dr. Martin Luther King, Jr. (1929-1968) became a great leader in the civil rights movement for three basic reasons. First, he popularized the use of nonviolent action to oppose the brutality and prejudice that African Americans faced in much of America. Second, he also stressed militancy, the need to actively oppose oppression. This part of his legacy is often forgotten by those who write about Dr. King. Third, he spread his message across the nation with an urgency, drama, and eloquence that few leaders have ever possessed. His great appeal as a communicator made him a superb spokesman for change.

In calling for a strict course of nonviolence, Dr. King had to contend with other prominent black leaders, including Malcolm X (1925-1965) who felt that "turning the other cheek" would only get it slapped. But Dr. King held that lasting social change could not be achieved by meeting violence with violence. That would achieve nothing but continued violence.

Although his is the name most connected to non-violent social protest, Martin Luther King, Jr. was not the first to use this method of achieving change. He was heavily influenced by Mohandas Gandhi (1869-1948), who used nonviolence to help India become independent from Britain.

Martin Luther King, Jr. stands in front of the State Capitol in Montgomery, Alabama, after completing a protest march in 1965 (*Wide World Photos*).

Dr. King led thousands of demonstrators to Washington, D.C. in 1963 during the March for Jobs and Freedom (*National Archives*).

But what about Dr. King's militancy? Nonviolent resistance is, after all, an active way of responding to injustice. It may be turning the other cheek, but it is not walking away. In fact, it's just the opposite. The heart of nonviolence is confrontation. It is saying to the oppressor: "Here is a mirror so you can see what you are doing, and who you are becoming." And this is what brought about the ideas presented in the following excerpt.

The Birmingham, Alabama police department, headed by Chief "Bull" Connor, shared the social views of much of the white South at the time. They expected blacks to defer to whites—to the point where a black person on a sidewalk was expected to move aside to let a white person pass. When black people in Birmingham demanded an end to segregation, the police used clubs, hoses, and dogs on them. As a leader in the protest, Dr. King was arrested.

White "moderate" ministers in the area called for an end to the demonstrations, implying that it was not the action of the police but the actions of the protestors that were the source of the problem. From his jail cell, Martin Luther King, Jr. wrote this famous letter to explain why the demonstrations were necessary.

Martin Luther King, Jr.: Letter from a Birmingham Jail

You deplore the demonstrations taking place in Birmingham. But your statement, I am sorry to say, fails to express a similar concern for the conditions that brought about the demonstrations.

You may well ask, "Why direct action? Why sit-ins, marches, and so forth? Isn't negotiation a better path?" You are quite right in calling for negotiation. Indeed, this is the very purpose of direct action. Nonviolent direct action seeks to create such a crisis and foster such a tension that a community which has constantly refused to negotiate is forced to confront the issue. It seeks to dramatize the issue so that it can no longer be ignored.

We know through painful experience that freedom is never voluntarily given by the oppressor. It must be demanded by the oppressed. Frankly, I have yet to engage in a direct-action campaign that was "well timed" in view of those who have not suffered unduly from the disease of segregation.

For years now I have heard the word "Wait!" It rings in the ear of every Negro with piercing familiarity. This "Wait!" has almost always meant

"Never." We must come to see, with one of our distinguished jurists, that "justice too long delayed is justice denied."

We have waited for more than 340 years for our constitutional and God-given rights. The nations of Asia and Africa are moving with jetlike speed toward gaining political independence, but we still creep at horse-and-buggy pace toward gaining a cup of coffee at a lunch counter. Perhaps it is easy for those who have never felt the stinging darts of segregation to say, "Wait."

I must make two honest confessions to you, my Christian and Jewish brothers. First, I must confess that over the past few years I have been gravely disappointed with the white moderate. I have almost reached the regrettable conclusion that the Negro's great stumbling block in his stride toward freedom is not the White Citizen's Councilor or the Ku Klux Klanner, but the white moderate, who is more devoted to "order" than to justice; who prefers a negative peace which is the absence of tension to a positive peace which is the presence of justice; who constantly says, "I agree with you in the goal you seek, but I cannot agree with your methods of direct action"; who paternalistically believes he can set the timetable for another man's freedom; who lives by a mythical concept of time and who constantly advises the Negro to wait for a "more convenient season."

Shallow understanding from people of good will is more frustrating than absolute misunderstanding from people of ill will. Luke-warm acceptance is much more bewildering than outright rejection.

From: *Why We Can't Wait* © 1963, 1964 by Martin Luther King, Jr. New York: Harper & Row Publishers, Inc. Reprinted by permission.

Malcolm X (*Library of Congress*).

The Minister from Harlem

When Spike Lee, a prominent film director and producer, released his film *Malcolm X* in 1992, it revived an interest in one of the most controversial figures of the 1960s. Suddenly, Malcolm X's picture appeared everywhere on T-shirts and posters. Baseball caps with an "X" on the front became one of the most stylish fashion items of the 1990s. *The Autobiography of Malcolm X*, published nearly 30 years earlier, became a bestseller again.

He was born Malcolm Little, in 1925. In 1946 he went to prison for burglary. While serving time, he met the Black Muslims, who were followers of Elijah Muhammad (1897-1975). This group's beliefs were similar to those of Marcus Garvey (1887-1940), who called for black nationalism in the 1920s. Like Garvey, the Muslims believed that blacks should not try to integrate with whites. Instead, the Muslims said blacks should establish their own homeland, open their own stores, even worship their own God (whose prophet Elijah Muhammad claimed to be). Their religion said that blacks were superior to whites.

Out of prison in 1952, Malcolm X, as he now called himself, became a Black Muslim minister. He was a powerful spokesperson. Malcolm X would preach on street corners or wherever blacks would stop to listen. He headed New York's Black Muslim temple, and eventually became the second-most powerful Black Muslim after Elijah Muhammad. His most important convert was boxing's heavyweight champion, Cassius Clay, who became known as Muhammad Ali.

In the 1960s, *The Autobiography of Malcolm X* made a deep impression on America. Written with Alex Haley (whose own story, *Roots*, became a best-seller and landmark TV miniseries), the book made a case for black nationalism and against nonviolence.

Malcolm X said that whites would never respect blacks unless blacks stood up for themselves and re-plied to violence in kind. He also preached that civil rights leaders who called for nonviolence no matter how blacks were treated were leading black people down a dangerous path. This philosophy essentially pitted Malcolm X against Martin Luther King, Jr.

In his book, Malcolm X also pointed out that other groups—immigrants from Europe, for example—had done well in America by setting up their own busi-nesses. They helped each other out by shopping in stores owned by "their own kind." African Americans, he believed, should do the same.

Although Malcolm X's and Dr. Martin Luther King, Jr.'s views were often used as examples of opposite approaches to civil rights, they were not entirely different. Each acted out of a love for his people. Martin Luther King, Jr. gradually became more militant as he saw that white resistance to change was stronger than he had first thought. Malcolm X, after a pilgrimage to the Middle East, returned with a new understanding of Islam and broke with the Black Muslims over the idea that whites were naturally evil. Finally, each man risked his personal safety for the cause of freedom for African Americans. In the end, both gave their lives to their cause, falling victim to bullets from the guns of assassins. Malcolm X was killed in New York City in 1965.

Malcolm X, Against Integration

The American black man should be focusing his every effort toward building his *own* businesses, and decent homes for himself. As other ethnic groups have done, let the black people, wherever possible, however possible, patronize their own kind, hire their own kind, and start in those ways to build up the black race's ability to do for itself. That's the only way the American black man is ever going to get respect. One thing the white man never can give the black man is self-respect! The black man never can become independent and recognized as a human being who is truly equal with other human beings until he has what they have, and until he is doing for himself what others are doing for themselves.

The black man in the ghettoes, for instance, has to start self-correcting his own material, moral, and spiritual defects and evils. The black man needs to start his own program to get rid of drunkenness, drug addiction, prostitution. The black man in America has to lift up his own sense of values.

If you want to get right down to the real outcome of this so-called "integration," what you've got to arrive at is intermarriage.

I'm right *with* the Southern white man who believes that you can't have so-called "integration," at least not for long, without intermarriage increasing. And what good is this for anyone? Let's again face reality. In a world as color-hostile as this, man or woman, black or white, what do they want with a mate of the other race?

Certainly white people have served enough notice of their hostility to any blacks in their families and neighborhoods. And the way most Negroes feel today, a mixed couple probably finds that black families, black communities, are even more hostile than the white ones. So what's bound to face "integrated" marriages, except being unwelcomed, unwanted "misfits" in whichever world they try to live in? What we arrive at is that "integration," socially, is no good for either side. "Integration," ultimately, would destroy the white race...and destroy the black race.

From: *The Autobiography of Malcolm X* by Malcolm X and Alex Haley (New York: Grove Press, 1965). Reprinted by permission.

CHAPTER 3

BUILDING A "GREAT SOCIETY"

Looking at America's Schools

Most Americans agreed in the early and mid-1960s that change was needed to make America a better society. The civil rights movement did much to cause this feeling. Articles in magazines, books, and television programs alerted America to the fact that decades of inequality had left African Americans at a great disadvantage in almost every aspect of life—for example, jobs, and health and education.

Given the desire to change, Americans then began to debate the best way to achieve it. Change cost money. But there was a limit to how much could be spent, and many people argued over how the money should be spent.

In the 1950s, national attention had centered on the schools. The Supreme Court's 1954 decision in

Brown v. *the Board of Education of Topeka* ordered that all schools be desegregated. This helped to spark civil rights activity on many fronts. In the 1960s, the nation again turned its eyes to the classroom.

With the new awareness of poverty and the struggles of black people in America, much was written describing what public schools were like in poor neighborhoods. The excerpt that follows comes from one of the most important accounts, Jonathan Kozol's *Death At An Early Age*. The title says a lot about what he thought of the Boston public schools where he taught during the 1964-1965 school year.

Kozol's account of what he saw shocked America. It was a portrait not of places where students failed, but rather of schools that were failing their students. Teachers in many of these schools had given up. They looked down on their pupils and the students knew it. Ghetto schools had come to reflect the attitude of much of society toward blacks and Latinos. Little was expected from them, so not much effort (or money) was put into their education. Their schools were allowed to decay and any problems students might have had because of the prejudice they faced were not dealt with.

Accounts like Kozol's came at a time when the idealism stirred up by President Kennedy's New Frontier was finally bearing fruit in government programs under President Lyndon B. Johnson's Great Society. The schools had an important place in these programs. It was thought that, if only the chains of poverty and prejudice could be broken early, students could grow up with a better view of themselves and be better qualified to live happy and productive lives. This, in turn, would help to reduce many of society's ills, including crime and poverty.

By the mid-1960s, the young people inspired by President Kennedy were beginning to graduate from college. Peace Corps volunteers were coming home after service abroad. Many of these people went into teaching. The government developed programs such as Head Start, which recognized that students living in poor areas had special needs. Looking back, not nearly as much change was accomplished as Americans had hoped, but the efforts did make a difference. People like Jonathan Kozol can be proud of themselves for their dedication.

The Failure in Education

The summer before I entered the school system, I had been working as a volunteer tutor in a Roxbury church. About a week after the class started, and after I had been told to admit no more pupils, a boy with the beard of a man appeared, about sixteen or seventeen, who turned out to be the older brother of one of the Fifth Grade pupils in the class. He could have been out playing, earning money, driving a car, doing anything he pleased. Instead he listened outside a volunteer tutor's make-shift class and at the end of each week he would ask me if there was any chance of someone's dropping out so that he could get in to take the empty place. He was in the Eighth Grade but he had never learned to read. People who talk about these things are often heard resorting to the explanation that it "all starts in the home" or else that "these people just don't want to learn." Whenever I hear that, I think of that boy who stood in the hallway outside the door of my classroom for an entire summer of hot and weary mornings, waiting there to walk his sisters home when they were finished and hoping that he might somehow be admitted to the sessions too. There was nothing wrong with his motivation, and there was nothing wrong in his home or homelife either. It was the public schools, pure and simple, which had held him back and made the situation of his life pathetic. It is the same story for thousands of other children all over Boston, and I believe it is the same for children in dozens of other cities in the United States too.

From: *Death At An Early Age* by Jonathan Kozol (Boston: Houghton Mifflin Company, 1967). Reprinted by permission.

Trying to Justify the War in Vietnam

Had it not been for Vietnam, Lyndon B. Johnson (1908-1973) would have been remembered as "the reform president," the man whose Great Society did more to help Americans than anything else that had come out of Washington since the New Deal. But bit by bit, through "escalation," he committed troops to the war until the daily war news almost blotted out everything else.

Johnson didn't start the war. America first got involved under President Eisenhower. President Kennedy increased the number of American "advisors" in Vietnam until the United States became part of what some people at the time thought was a Vietnamese civil war. Many Americans said it was a conflict in which we had no business getting involved, but Johnson sent several hundred thousand troops into what soon became a full-scale—but undeclared—war.

Opponents of the war charged that the government of South Vietnam, which America had befriended, was a corrupt regime that its people justly hated. People asked, "Why, then, are we there?"

In April 1965, Johnson made one of his first major speeches defending U.S. involvement in Vietnam, excerpted in the following passage. He spoke of the war in Asia against the backdrop of the Cold War and said the United States had to defend any threat to freedom. Not to do so, he asserted, would encourage Communists to try to take over other countries, and there would then be no end to conflict. If one Asian country fell to the Communists, the theory went, others would topple as well—like falling dominoes.

But Johnson did not count on the eroding effect that TV was having on support for the war. In the past, the government had carefully controlled news from the battlefield. Now reporters and camerapeople were in the foxholes with the troops and interviewing South Vietnamese villagers whose homes—and, sometimes, children—had been accidentally hit by American bombs. The pictures also vividly showed the death of American soldiers and the conditions under which they had to live and fight in this foreign land. Brought into America's living rooms this way, the war, to many, did not seem nearly as necessary as the president made it out to be.

American soldiers turn away from a South Vietnamese home as it burns (*Wide World Photos*).

Lyndon B. Johnson on Why We Are in Vietnam

Tonight Americans and Asians are dying for a world where each people may choose its own path to change.

This is the principle for which our ancestors fought in the valleys of Pennsylvania. It is the principle for which our sons fight tonight in the jungles of Vietnam.

Vietnam is far away from this quiet campus. We have no territory there, nor do we seek any. The war is dirty and brutal and difficult. And some 400 young men, born into an America that is bursting with opportunity and promise, have ended their lives on Vietnam's steaming soil.

Why must we take this painful road?

The first reality is that North Vietnam has attacked the independent nation of South Vietnam. Its object is total conquest.

Of course, some of the people of South Vietnam are participating in attack on their own government. But trained men and supplies, orders and arms, flow in a constant stream from north to south.

Over this war—and all Asia—is another reality: the deepening shadow of Communist China. The rulers in Hanoi are urged on by Peking. This is a regime which has destroyed freedom in Tibet, which has attacked India, and has been condemned by the United Nations for aggression in Korea. It is a nation which is helping the forces of violence in almost every continent. The contest in Vietnam is part of a wider pattern of aggressive purposes.

Why are these realities our concern? Why are we in South Vietnam?

We are there because we have a promise to keep. Since 1954 every American President has offered support to the people of South Vietnam. We have helped to build, and we have helped to defend. Thus, over many years, we have made a national pledge to help South Vietnam defend its independence. . . .

We are also there to strengthen world order. Around the globe, from Berlin to Thailand, are people whose well-being rests, in part, on the belief that they can count on us if they are attacked. To leave Vietnam to its fate would shake the confidence of all these people in the value of an American commitment and in the value of America's word. The result would be increased unrest and instability, and even wider war.

We are also there because there are great stakes in the balance. Let no one think for a moment that retreat from Vietnam would bring an end to conflict. The battle would be renewed in one country and then another. The central lesson of our time is that the appetite of aggression is never satisfied. To withdraw from one battlefield means only to prepare for the next. We must say in southeast Asia—as we did in Europe—in the words of the Bible: "Hitherto shalt thou come, but no further."

From: Lyndon Baines Johnson, "Peace Without Conquest," Address at Johns Hopkins University, April 7, 1965, Department of State Bulletin, April 26, 1965.

Families with sons in Vietnam got letters at home describing what the war was really like. There seemed to be more confusion than heroism and glory. As the excerpt from the following firsthand account makes clear, soldiers could never be really sure of just who the enemy was. Sometimes this confusion led to great tragedy. Dave Baker, the soldier whose account is excerpted here, was on patrol in a South Vietnamese village with a guard dog. The VC (Vietcong) were the Communist guerilla fighters, who the GIs couldn't tell from the friendly South Vietnamese.

American soldiers move across an open field in Vietnam (*Wide World Photos*).

A Soldier Remembers

The dog handler's job was to patrol the bush outside the village at night to make sure none of the VC [Vietcong] could sneak up on us. There were tunnels around our unit, and the VC would use them to get close to the fence. Then they'd come up and through the fence and get to our main communications center. Tried to blow it up a number of times.

In the village I was in and in the villages around, there were just local VC. They'd have maybe two or three bullets allotted to them to shoot for the night, and they'd come out with their single-shot rifles and go *blinkety-blink*. About every two weeks or so, they'd put on a mortar attack, but primarily it was just snipers. You always had to watch your back, because there was no front line there, and you had women and kids as warriors, too, and you really didn't know who was trustworthy and who wasn't. It was all a battlefield.

There'd be accidents, bad accidents. In one village that I had to go through, the kids would play a game: They would try to touch the killer dogs. If they could touch a killer dog, they were big heroes. But this wasn't known to me when I first got there. A lot of the old-timers don't tell you all the tricks of the trade, you know. So I knew nothing of this game of the kids. One night I was working, cutting through the side of the village, and I'm looking into a shack over there and I see a bunch of eyes. I didn't know whose they were. I just figured to myself, Jesus, somebody in there is going to shoot me just when I get to the right spot.

I had my gun on my side with my hand on it, and my dog was pulling ahead real hard, but I wasn't paying too much attention to him. I was looking at those eyes as I walked. And I was on the ready, because if I saw anything that looked wrong, I was going to start shooting. What I didn't know was that those eyes were all little kids watching their buddy, who had dug a ditch and hidden himself under some weeds right by the path. When I came by, he was going to jump up, touch my dog, and then take off, and he would be a hero. And they were watching for him to do it. So as I went by, he jumped up, touched my dog, and my dog took his head off instantly. [*Sharp snap of fingers.*] Just popped it like that. You know, some of these Vietnam people are very, very thin, especially the young kids. The neck was like a dog bone to him.

I didn't know what to do. I mean, I'm standing there—the head's sitting over there, spitting and gurgling. Oooooh.... I get goose bumps now just think about it. It was a real ripper for me. I pulled the dog back quick, and I looked this way and that way, and the kid's mother was coming after me. She had something in her hand, and I thought, "It's a grenade. It's cocked. I'm in real trouble now." So I had to pack her down. I shot her. We can't take a gamble, you know. I just blasted her, and I kept shooting as I backed out.

When I got back to my base, they sent an alert out to see what went on, and it turned out she just had a rock in her hand, but I didn't know that. I just thought, She's going to get me, and I'm going to blast her....

And, you know, it stays with you. When you're that close to them, and you see it happen—it's not like when you're in the dark, and you're shooting, and the next day you hear that somebody fell down dead. Here, you're with them, and you see it, and it stays with you. I imagine a lot of guys who were there don't mention things like that to anybody. They keep it in, because it's hurting them, and it hurts them to keep it in, too.

From: *From Camelot to Kent State: The Sixties Experience in the Words of Those Who Lived It* by Joan Morrison and Robert K. Morrison, pp. 61-65, 67-70, 76-81. Copyright © 1987 by Joan Morrison and Robert K. Morrison. Reprinted by permission of Times Books, a division of Random House, Inc.

Protesting the War in Asia

It took a while for the reaction to the Vietnam War to reach the fever pitch it did for some. Although, at first, the protests against the war were very orderly and respectable, they soon became more disruptive and then violent.

The demonstrations started on college campuses with "teach-ins." These were mass meetings in which people spoke out on their feelings about the war and where others came to get information. Around 1965, marches were beginning to take place. Held locally, they often ended at symbolic places, such as the local army recruiting center. The protestors also marched on Washington. The first antiwar protest rally in the capital in 1965 drew about 25,000 people. Besides listening to speeches and songs, the crowd chanted: "Stop the bombing, end the war, bring the troops home."

Imitating the civil rights movement, some of the most dedicated protestors nonviolently resisted the war by chaining themselves to the door of an army recruitment center, for example. Another form of protest that became popular was the burning of draft cards by young men who were required by law to carry them at all times. Men who were drafted and refused to go to Vietnam often fled to Canada to avoid imprisonment.

As time went on frustration grew with the rise in the number of American troops in Vietnam. As more Americans arrived, bombing campaigns were also stepped up and the demonstrations at home took on a new, more urgent, tone. Chants of "Hey, hey, LBJ, how

many kids did you kill today?" were often heard. Sometimes protestors burned the American flag.

Despite the growing anger, most demonstrations were still orderly. But they were getting bigger, and by 1967, U.S. representatives and senators were speaking at demonstrations as opposition to the war became more widespread and accepted. Martin Luther King, Jr. spoke at one antiwar march.

Jerry Rubin, a political activist who regularly organized demonstrations, made a threat that is clear in the excerpt that follows. His statement was a taste of things to come. The most radical wing of the antiwar

Antiwar protests were common throughout the 1960s. Thousands gathered in Boston in 1969 to protest the war in Vietnam (© *Costa Manos, Magnum*).

movement, which included Students for a Democratic Society (SDS), felt that the only way to end the war was to make the cost of continuing it too great to bear. If Johnson would not pull out, these radicals decided, there should be chaos in the streets and a general undermining of "things as usual" until the troops came home. For many, the slogan now became, "From Protest to Resistance."

There was chaos in the streets of Chicago in August 1968 when the Democrats held their election-year convention. Did the demonstrators accomplish anything? That question is still debated. The strong language in the following passage is proof of just how emotional the issue of war became in the 1960s.

In an act of defiance, Jerry Rubin publicly burns a subpoena to appear before the House Un-American Activities Committee in 1968 (*Wide World Photos*).

Jerry Rubin Lights a Fuse of Antiwar Feeling

There are thousands of young people in this country who want to get the "white man" out of us, who choose the lot of the oppressed in the world. This system lives by murdering in Vietnam, exploiting the world, and killing black people at home; and we say to hell with the middle class "security" and phony status games, we are going to screw up this society.

And we can do it too. We can force Johnson to bring the 82nd Airborne Division and 100,000 more troops to Chicago next August to protect the Democratic National Convention. With luck, Johnson will get himself nominated under military guard. We can disrupt the traffic of America's major cities. Who knows—some night, a draft board may just disappear.

The white rebellion is on. An alive section of the peace movement—mostly its under-35 group—is realizing that what we need is not a peace movement, but a movement for liberation. Fighting American involvement in Vietnam is the same as liberating ourselves from privileged positions in a sick society based on a racist and selfish morality.

From: "We Are Going to Light the Fuse to the Bomb" by Jerry Rubin. (New York: *The Village Voice*, November 16, 1967.) Reprinted by permission.

CHAPTER 4

A CULTURE OF COUNTERCULTURE

Dr. Timothy Leary promoted the use of drugs in the 1960s as a means of mind expansion (© *Gamma-Liaison*).

The Growth of Drug Use

"Turn on, tune in, drop out," was the advice from former Harvard professor Timothy Leary to the youth of America in the 1960s. He was talking to students and others not about their ABC's but about LSD, a very powerful drug that caused hallucinations and other "mind-bending" experiences.

In the 1960s, a revolution in the use of drugs occurred in America, mostly among people under the age of 30. In the years before, nothing stronger than alcohol would have been found in middle-class schools and neighborhoods. Now, at social events, young people passed around "joints" (marijuana cigarettes). In certain areas such as college towns where there were many young people, "pot" might be smoked openly, on the street, even though it was illegal to do so. Marijuana had almost become as common with young people as cigarettes.

Many people in popular culture romanticized marijuana and hallucinogens, such as LSD. The Beatles, for example, sang about LSD in their song, "Lucy in the Sky with Diamonds," and about drug use in "Fixing a Hole," on their groundbreaking album, *Sgt. Pepper's Lonely Hearts Club Band*. The poet Allen Ginsberg traveled around the country speaking about how drugs would make people lose their reserve and feel freer and more peaceful.

There were stories about teenagers "freaking out" on bad LSD "trips." The drug was usually taken on a sugar cube, and too many people took it as if it was candy. Sometimes people ended up in hospital emergency rooms, and sometimes they died.

In the following excerpt, Duke D. Fisher, M.D., a neuropsychiatrist, recalls the many young patients he treated because of bad LSD "trips."

A Doctor Describes the Dangers of LSD

We started seeing many young people coming to our hospital at UCLA because of bad trips. We studied the first seventy patients who came to our emergency room to find out what kind of symptoms they had with their bad trips. The most common symptoms we found were the same as those of people suffering from a persistent psychosis, those who live in an unreal world. Some people would take LSD and their trip would continue beyond the usual twelve to eighteen hours for LSD effects. Many individuals continued to hallucinate, continued to be paranoid—extremely suspicious with delusions of being watched, criticized, or persecuted. They were convinced that people were going to hurt them or that animals were chasing them, or they continued to be out of contact with reality. An example of this kind of reaction was a teenage boy who locked himself in his room because he thought he was an orange and that if someone touched him, he would turn into orange juice. He was able to live because a few friends would bring in food for him; however, he remained locked in his room for several months. This type of false belief is called a delusion. We found delusions to be quite common among young people who had taken LSD. The second most common symptom was severe depression—many times with suicidal thoughts. We talked to many young people who were convinced they had to die because they felt so unworthy. One young girl broke a Coke bottle and cut both of her wrists after she had taken LSD at a Hollywood nightclub. Some individuals are successful in their suicide attempts. The third most common symptom we saw in the emergency room was anxiety to the point of panic. Many people would become quite frightened at the fact that they were losing control of themselves under LSD. One college student had taken LSD and had an accident on the freeway. He was so anxious that he ran up and down the freeway until the police were able to restrain him and bring him to our hospital for treatment. The last, most commonly observed symptom was confusion or wandering about. Many LSD users were brought to our hospital not knowing where they were going or who they were. Some of these people would be found wandering around beaches or the city at night. Many of them were malnourished and had physical difficulties because of long exposure to the sun.

From: *Mind Drugs* edited by Margaret O. Hyde (New York: Dodd, Mead & Co., 1986.)

Questioning American Values

The 1960s were a time of another kind of protest besides the ones that questioned the war in Vietnam and the treatment of African Americans. Many Americans in their teens and 20s had come to feel uneasy about accepted social standards in the United States. They protested the tone of the whole culture—the way people worked and prepared for careers, the schools, the way everyone was expected to dress, and the other things that most Americans assumed were part of "the good life." This protest had its roots in the "anti-establishment" Beatnik movement of the 1950s, when people dropped out of society to live a freer and less materialistic life.

The new 1960s protestors felt that there was too much respect for authority, too much censorship of people's natural feelings in matters such as sex, and too many restrictions on "mind-expanding" practices such as the use of drugs. These youths wanted more freedom in every aspect of life. People called the loose "movement" that formed around these issues the "counterculture." Those who were most willing to act on their desire for freedom were called "hippies."

What was middle-class America to think of men with long hair, men and women walking barefoot in the streets, young women who moved in with their boyfriends, people smoking marijuana, the spread of loud rock music with explicit lyrics, and bumper stickers and buttons that said "Don't Trust Anyone Over 30" and "All You Need Is Love"?

"Hippies" dressed in brightly colored clothes as a way to express their desire to be "different" (*Bettmann Archives*).

The hippies didn't seem bothered by the reaction of their parents' generation. In fact, they sometimes seemed to enjoy the upheaval they were causing.

The spring and summer of 1967 saw the hippies at their peak. In New York's Central Park, hippies held a huge "Be-In," described in the following excerpt by Don McNeill, a free-lance journalist. As summer approached, the title of a hit song said it all: "Are You Going to San Francisco?" That city's Haight-Asbury neighborhood became the hippie capital of America during this "summer of love."

Even though the hippies eventually faded, their revolution left a strong mark. Bankers, lawyers, and truck drivers began to let their hair grow. Even straight-laced business people began to dress with more flair.

Hippies sit together on a beach in Honolulu, Hawaii (*Wide World Photos*).

The spirit of liberation also helped to spark movements for women's equality, gay rights, and environmental preservation. Sexual values became liberalized. Though the counterculture was first ridiculed and dismissed as "silly," it had actually made an enormous impact.

Looking Back on the "Summer of Love"

As the dawn sun gleamed off a backdrop of molded metal skyscrapers on Easter Sunday, a medieval pageant began in the middle of Manhattan. Laden with daffodils, ecstatic in vibrant costumes and painted faces, troupes of hippies gathered on a hill overlooking Central Park's Sheep Meadow to Be-In. By sunset, ten thousand celebrants swarmed in great rushes across the meadow, and thousands more were dispersed throughout the rest of the park. Bonfires burned on the hills, their smoke mixing with bright balloons among the barren trees and high, high above kites wafted in the air. Rhythms and music and mantras from all corners of the meadow echoed in exquisite harmony, and thousands of lovers vibrated into the night. It was miraculous.

It was a feast for the senses: the beauty of the colors, clothes, and shrines, the sounds and the rhythms, at once familiar, the smell of flowers and frankincense, the taste of jellybeans. But the spirit of the Be-In penetrated beneath the senses, deep into instincts. The Be-In was tuned—in time—to past echoes and future premonitions. Layers of inhibitions were peeled away and, for many, love and laughter became suddenly fresh.

People climbed into trees and made animal calls, and were answered by calls from other trees. Two men stripped naked, and were gently persuaded to reclothe as the police appeared. Herds of people rushed together from encampments on the hills to converge *en masse* on the great mud of the meadow. They joined hands to form great circles, hundreds of yards in diameter, and broke to hurtle to the center in a joyous, crushing, multiembracing pigpile. Chains of people careened through the crowds at full run. Their energy seemed inexhaustible.

The password was "LOVE" and it was sung, chanted, painted across foreheads, and spelled out on costumes. A tall man, his face painted white, wearing a silk top hat adorned with straw flowers, wandered through the Be-In holding aloft a tiny sign reading "LOVE."

The Police and Parks departments quietly and unofficially cooperated with the Be-Ins. A police car arrived shortly before seven in the morning and the few hundred people already gathered rushed the car and pelted it with flowers, yelling, "Daffodil Power." The police, astonished and covered with flowers, beat a hasty retreat.

"The police were beautiful," said Jim Fouratt, who helped to organize the Be-In. "It was really strange and it freaked them out, but they were beautiful."

From: *Moving Through Here* by Don McNeill (New York: Knopf, 1970). Reprinted by permission.

Seeking Equal Rights for Women

For society as a whole, few questions could be more basic than "Where and what is a woman's place?" In 1968, some thought it was in the home and one step behind her husband. Others thought a woman's place was anywhere her ambition and abilities could take her. Redefining women's roles, it seemed, could rock the very foundations of American society. What would making women the equal of men do to the nuclear family where the man was the breadwinner and the woman was the homemaker and mother?

The new "feminists" answered the doubters by saying *everyone* would lead better lives if women were free to do more. Liberating women would free men as well, they said, because men had been oppressors even if they didn't know it.

Although many ideas of modern feminism date from the nineteenth century, they really blossomed early in the twentieth century, with the movement to secure the vote for women in the 1920s. A number of factors contributed to this change. Modern appliances made it easier to take care of housework. More jobs for women took many of them outside the home. A generally freer and more questioning atmosphere in society allowed women to better assert themselves.

The publication of Betty Friedan's (1921-) book, *The Feminine Mystique*, in 1963 is often said to mark the beginning of the modern women's movement in this country. But the movement didn't pick up steam until the late 1960s. In the wake of all the other protest

America's foremost women's leaders led a march to the Capitol in Washington, D.C. in 1978. Shown above are (left to right) Bella Abzug, Gloria Steinem, Dick Gregory, Betty Friedan, Representative Barbara Mikulski, and Representative Margaret Heckler. (The woman far right is unidentified.) (*Wide World Photos*).

movements, women began to demonstrate for equal rights. Gradually, the movement became more accepted and more widespread.

Gloria Steinem (1934-   ) was a pioneer in the women's movement—a "founding mother." The magazine she helped to start, *Ms.*, popularized a new form of address for women and helped the nation question its old ideas about women. In the following excerpt, from 1970, Steinem is testifying at a Senate hearing in favor of an Equal Rights Amendment to the Constitution, known as ERA. This amendment, which would have constitutionally guaranteed equality for women, was passed by Congress but was not ratified by enough states, and therefore did not become a law.

Still, in the more than two decades since Steinem gave this testimony, local and state laws, and the provisions of specific acts of Congress, have enacted much of what the amendment would have done. Changes in business practices and the values we live by have also resulted in great strides towards equal rights for women.

Gloria Steinem Speaks to Congress

My name is Gloria Steinem. I am a writer and editor, and I am currently a member of the policy council of the Democratic committee. And I work regularly with the lowest-paid workers in the country, the migrant workers, men, women, and children both in California and in my own State of New York.

During 12 years of working for a living, I have experienced much of the legal and social discrimination reserved for women in this country. I have been refused service in public restaurants, ordered out of public gathering places, and turned away from apartment rentals; all for the clearly-stated, sole reason that I am a woman. And all without the legal remedies available to blacks and other minorities. I have been excluded from professional groups, writing assignments on so-called "unfeminine" subjects such as politics, full participation in the Democratic Party, jury duty, and even from such small male privileges as discounts on airline fares. Most important to me, I have been denied a society in which women are encouraged, or even allowed to think of themselves as first-class citizens and responsible human beings.

However, after two years of researching the status of American women, I have discovered that in reality, I am very, very lucky. Most women, both wage-earners and housewives, routinely suffer more humiliation and injustice than I do.

As a freelance writer, I don't work in the male-dominated hierarchy of an office. (Women, like blacks and other visibly different minorities, do better in individual professions such as the arts, sports, or domestic work; anything in which they don't have authority over white male.) I am not one of the millions of women who must support a family. Therefore, I haven't had to go on welfare because there are no day-care centers for my children while I work, and I haven't had to submit to the humiliating welfare inquiries about my private and sexual life, inquires from which men are exempt. I haven't had to brave the sex bias of labor unions and employers, only to see my family subsist on a median salary 40 percent less than the male median salary.

I hope this committee will hear the personal, daily injustices suffered by many women—professionals and day laborers, women house-bound by welfare as well as by suburbia. We have all been silent for too long. But we won't be silent anymore.

From: "The Equal Rights" Amendment: Hearings Before the Subcommittee on Constitutional Amendments of the Committee of the Judiciary of the United States Senate, 91st Congress, May 5, 6, and 7, 1970 (Washington, D.C., Government Printing Office, 1970).

CHAPTER 5

THE "BROKEN PACT"

Speaking for the "Silent Majority"

By the fall of 1968, after several years of student protests, hippies, and riots in the nation's black ghettos, much of America felt as if it had "had enough." "The silent majority," as candidate Richard Nixon (1913-   ) called the older generation, wanted peace and quiet and a return to old values. They wanted someone to put the lid on constant change and disruption.

Nixon's campaign slogan assured them: "Nixon's the One." The candidate gave the job of verbally attacking hippie protestors and lawbreakers to Spiro Agnew (1918–   ), the man he had chosen for his running mate. By doing this, Nixon could leave fighting the hard and messy battle to Agnew.

As a candidate, and then as vice-president, Agnew went out of his way to taunt protestors, whipping up crowds by calling the rebels all sorts of names. The targets of his attacks responded with total contempt

Richard Nixon (right) and Spiro Agnew were the Republican nominees for president and vice-president at the 1968 national convention (*Wide World Photos*).

for him, his party, and the government he represented. Now more than at any other time, progressives of all kinds—especially young people—felt totally separated from the administration in Washington. It was simply not their government.

Now there appeared to be two Americas. And in the excerpt from a 1969 speech that follows, Agnew seems to be aiming at making the split complete. He even calls for "polarization." That is, he wants people to draw away from the middle toward either end of the political spectrum. "You're either with us or against us," he was saying.

In a twist of history, this man who was so quick to criticize law-breaking hippies, was forced to resign the vice-presidency because he broke the law. While governor of Maryland, and even when he was the vice-president, he accepted payoffs from construction companies to get them favorable treatment on government contracts. Agnew resigned his post in disgrace on October 10, 1973.

Spiro Agnew Lashes Out

Think about it. Small bands of students are allowed to shut down great universities. Small groups of dissidents are allowed to shout down political candidates. Small cadres of professional protestors are allowed to jeopardize the peace efforts of the President of the United States.

It is time to question the credentials of their leaders. And, if in questioning we disturb a few people, I say it is time for them to be disturbed. If, in challenging, we polarize the American people, I say it is time for a positive polarization.

Now, we have among us a glib, activist element who would tell us our values are lies, and I call them impudent. Because anyone, who impugns a legacy of liberty and dignity that reaches back to Moses, is impudent.

I call them snobs for most of them disdain to mingle with the masses who work for a living. They mock the common man's pride in his work, his family, and his country. It has also been said that I called them intellectuals. I did not. I said that they characterized themselves as intellectuals. No true intellectual, no truly knowledgeable person, would so despise democratic institutions.

America cannot afford to write off a whole generation for the decadent thinking of a few. We can, however, afford to separate them from our society—with no more regret than we should feel over discarding rotten apples from a barrel.

From: "Impudence in the Streets" Address at Pennsylvania Republican Dinner by Spiro Agnew, Harrisburg, October 30, 1969.

Tragedy at Kent State

D emonstrations against the Vietnam War continued throughout the late 1960s. On November 15, 1969, about 250,000 protestors went to Washington to pressure the government to end the war. The next day, newspapers reported that U.S. soldiers had massacred unarmed men, women, and children at the town of My Lai. A wave of antiwar public opinion swept across the nation. Richard Nixon, now president, knew that he would have to do something to get America out of the conflict.

Nixon said that he would begin a policy of "Vietnamization," in which the United States would turn the fighting over to its South Vietnamese allies as U.S. troops were brought home. Meanwhile, however, the president stepped up the fighting. For the first time, he allowed U.S. soldiers to cross into neighboring Cambodia to go after the Communists. He also approved the bombing of Cambodia.

The spread of fighting to Cambodia made those who opposed the war even angrier. In May 1970, college campuses erupted with demonstrations against this expansion of the war. At Kent State University in Kent, Ohio, student protest had focused on the school's Reserve Officers Training Corps (R.O.T.C.) program. On May 3, demonstrators burned down the R.O.T.C. building on campus and the National Guard was called to the school.

The following day, student demonstrators clashed with the soldiers. Some students threw rocks. The

One of the four students killed by National Guard soldiers at Kent State lies dead as a fellow student grieves (*Wide World Photos*).

soldiers opened fire, killing four students and leaving nine wounded.

A stirring photograph of a young woman kneeling grief-stricken over the body of a fellow Kent State student appeared on the front pages of newspapers all over the country the next day. On May 14, state police killed two more protesting students on the campus of Jackson State College in Mississippi.

The killings horrified many Americans who had not even expressed strong opinions on the war. Most people thought this kind of violence was something that only happened in other countries, not here.

The excerpt that follows, by a Kent State first-year student, gives some sense of what it was like to have been at the Kent State demonstrations.

Reliving the Chaos of 1970

I woke up to the sound of gunfire. It sounded like—you know, when you sit in your backyard and fireworks are going off on the Fourth of July? That's what it sounded like. A few minutes later, my roommates came back in, and they were bawling their eyes out. They were very upset, and I said, "What happened?" They said, "There was a shooting on the commons. People were killed." All they knew was what had happened as they were running off. They didn't have any of the details. They were scared, and they were crying.

A few minutes later we heard the police coming through with their megaphones, saying "You must leave the campus immediately. Leave within a hour. Don't take anything. Just get out of here." It was like a police state. Later we learned that the dorms were searched and they confiscated a lot of weapons. They put it in the press that they found weapons, but they didn't find revolvers, they didn't find machine guns. They found knives, things like that, and, of course, they found a lot of joints, and the press made a big issue of that. They wanted to make us out to be radicals. But we weren't radicals at Kent State. They were radical at Berkeley, you know, but Kent State was just a mild school.

From: *From Camelot to Kent State: The Sixties Experience in the Words of Those Who Lived It* by Joan Morrison and Robert K. Morrison, pp. 61-65, 67-70, 76-81. Copyright © 1987 by Joan Morrison and Robert K. Morrison. Reprinted by permission of Times Books, a division of Random House, Inc.

Scandal in the White House

Watergate was different from other Washington scandals. For the very first time, the president of the United States seemed to be at the center of the crime. Just how much involvement Richard Nixon actually had in the criminal activities remains unclear even to this day.

First word of the scandal reached the public on June 18, 1972, during Nixon's campaign for a second term in the White House. Newspapers, TV, and radio reported that five men had been caught trying to break into the Democratic party's national headquarters in the Watergate building complex in Washington, D.C. At first, the story was reported as a fairly common burglary. But soon, the facts revealed a much more dramatic truth.

Gradually, evidence pointed to a connection between the burglars and The Committee to Re-elect the President. *Washington Post* reporters Carl Bernstein and Bob Woodward were responsible for uncovering much of this new information. For the next few months, Nixon managed to keep the issue in the background, and he was re-elected.

As soon as the "burglars" went on trial in January 1973, however, a torrent of incriminating facts burst onto the front pages of America's newspapers. It seemed that nearly every day Americans heard about a new connection between the crime and the president. Some of Nixon's top advisors, H.R. Haldeman and John Ehrlichman, were forced to resign. The Senate began

President Richard Nixon announced his resignation on August 8, 1974 (*Wide World Photos*).

an official investigation, supervised by Senator Sam Ervin.

In July came the biggest surprise of all. Nixon had put a taping system in his office that had recorded whatever was said there. A legal battle to get these tapes followed. As transcripts of the tapes were released, the country learned about more than just a burglary. Americans got a close look at a president who had an "enemies list" and a basic disregard for the law in pursuing those he considered "out to get" him.

The Watergate affair kept getting bigger and bigger. Attorney General John Mitchell soon had to resign. President Nixon wouldn't give up some of his tapes. Then he said an important 18-minute part of one of them had been "accidentally" erased. As president, Nixon had the power to fire the independent prosecutor who was investigating the Watergate affair.

In the March 21, 1973 excerpt from the Nixon tapes that follows, John Dean ("D"), Nixon's lawyer, is discussing with the president ("P"), how to make sure that the Watergate burglars don't start talking. Nixon and Dean were not above talking about bribery.

A "Private" Conversation in the Oval Office

D—So where are the soft spots on this? Well, first of all, there is the problem of the continued blackmail which will not only go on now, but it will go on while these people are in prison, and it will compound the obstruction of justice situation. It will cost money. It is dangerous. People around here are not pros at this sort of thing. This is the sort of thing Mafia people can do: washing money, getting clean money, and things like that. We just don't know about those things, because we are not criminals and not used to dealing in that business.

P—That's right.

D—It is a tough thing to know how to do.

P—Maybe it takes a gang to do that.

D—That's right. There is a real problem as to whether we could even do it. Plus there is a real problem in raising money. Mitchell has been working on raising some money. He is one of the ones with the most to lose. But there is no denying the fact that the White House, in Ehrlichman, Haldeman and Dean are involved in some of the early money decisions.

P—How much money do you need?

D—I would say these people are going to cost a million dollars over the next two years.

P—We could get that. On the money, if you need the money you could get that. You could get a million dollars. You could get it in cash. I know where it could be gotten. It is not easy, but it could be done. But the question is who the hell would handle it? Any ideas on that?

D—That's right. Well, I think that is something that Mitchell ought to be charged with.

P—I would think so too.

D—And get some pros to help him.

P—Let me say there shouldn't be a lot of people running around getting money—

From: Transcription of Watergate Tapes, March 21, 1973 (10:12–11:55 A.M.). Published by the Government Printing Office, Washington, D.C.

Finally, in August 1974, faced with the threat of removal by impeachment, Nixon became the first president of the United States ever to resign. In his place, Gerald R. Ford (1913–   ), who had replaced Spiro Agnew following his resignation, became president after serving as vice-president for only 10 months.

The most lasting effect of Watergate was a diminished respect for government and a general mistrust of public officials that many Americans still feel today. From that point on, the public would never think of the president as a person immune to corruption, greed, or the abuse of power.

1960

John F. Kennedy is elected president. In his inaugural address, he inspires young Americans to serve their country.

1962

The Cuban Missile Crisis pushes America and the Soviet Union to the brink of nuclear war.

1963–1968

America looses four leaders to assassins' bullets: John F. Kennedy, Malcolm X, Martin Luther King, Jr., and Robert Kennedy.

1963

Lyndon B. Johnson is sworn in as president. His "Great Society" enacts programs to help impoverished U.S. citizens.

1965–1969

Demonstrations against the Vietnam War grow. Washington D.C. sees protestors increase from 25,000 to 250,000 in four years.

1970

Fighting from the Vietnam War spreads to Cambodia. An antiwar protest at Kent State University leaves four dead.

1972–1973

The Watergate scandal rocks the capital. Nixon advisors are implicated and forced to quit their offices.

1973

Vice-President Spiro Agnew resigns after it is discovered that he accepted payoffs. Gerald R. Ford is appointed vice-president.

1974

Unable to clarify his role in the Watergate scandal, Nixon is threatened with impeachment. He becomes the first U.S. president to resign.

FOR FURTHER READING

Anderson, Catherine C. *John F. Kennedy*. Minneapolis: Lerner, 1991.

Archer, Jules. *The Incredible Sixties: The Stormy Years That Changed America*. San Diego: Harcourt Brace Jovanovich Juvenile Books, 1986.

Barr, Roger. *The Vietnam War*. San Diego: Lucent Books, 1991.

Darby, Jean. *Martin Luther King, Jr*. Minneapolis: Lerner, 1990.

Devaney, John. *Lyndon Baines Johnson, President*. New York: Walker & Co., 1986.

Hargrove, Jim. *Richard M. Nixon: Thirty-Seventh President*. Chicago: Children's Press, 1985.

Hoff, Mark. *Gloria Steinem: The Women's Movement*. Brookfield, CT: Millbrook Press, 1991.

Kosof, Anna. *The Civil Rights Movement and Its Legacy*. New York: Watts, 1989.

Lawson, Don. *The United States in the Vietnam War*. New York: HarperCollins Children's Books, 1981.

Powledge, Fred. *We Shall Overcome: Heroes of the Civil Rights Movement*. New York: Macmillan's Children Book Group, 1993.

Rowland, Della. *Martin Luther King, Jr.: The Dream of Peaceful Revolution*. Morristown, NJ: Silver Burdett, 1990.

Rummel, Jack. *Malcolm X*. New York: Chelsea House, 1989.

Weitsman, Madeline. *The Peace Corps*. New York: Chelsea House, 1989.

INDEX

973.9   Brown, Gene.
BRO
         The nation in
           turmoil.

$15.98

DATE			